The Left-Hander's 2025 Calendar

Left-Handed Legends, Lore & More

- Planning Pages on the Left
- Easier for Left-Handers to Use

BY CARY KOEGLE

Andrews McMeel
PUBLISHING®

2025

January
S	M	T	W	T	F	S
			1	2	3	4
5	6	7	8	9	10	11
12	13	14	15	16	17	18
19	20	21	22	23	24	25
26	27	28	29	30	31	

February
S	M	T	W	T	F	S
						1
2	3	4	5	6	7	8
9	10	11	12	13	14	15
16	17	18	19	20	21	22
23	24	25	26	27	28	

March
S	M	T	W	T	F	S
						1
2	3	4	5	6	7	8
9	10	11	12	13	14	15
16	17	18	19	20	21	22
23	24	25	26	27	28	29
30	31					

April
S	M	T	W	T	F	S
		1	2	3	4	5
6	7	8	9	10	11	12
13	14	15	16	17	18	19
20	21	22	23	24	25	26
27	28	29	30			

May
S	M	T	W	T	F	S
				1	2	3
4	5	6	7	8	9	10
11	12	13	14	15	16	17
18	19	20	21	22	23	24
25	26	27	28	29	30	31

June
S	M	T	W	T	F	S
1	2	3	4	5	6	7
8	9	10	11	12	13	14
15	16	17	18	19	20	21
22	23	24	25	26	27	28
29	30					

July
S	M	T	W	T	F	S
		1	2	3	4	5
6	7	8	9	10	11	12
13	14	15	16	17	18	19
20	21	22	23	24	25	26
27	28	29	30	31		

August
S	M	T	W	T	F	S
					1	2
3	4	5	6	7	8	9
10	11	12	13	14	15	16
17	18	19	20	21	22	23
24	25	26	27	28	29	30
31						

September
S	M	T	W	T	F	S
	1	2	3	4	5	6
7	8	9	10	11	12	13
14	15	16	17	18	19	20
21	22	23	24	25	26	27
28	29	30				

October
S	M	T	W	T	F	S
			1	2	3	4
5	6	7	8	9	10	11
12	13	14	15	16	17	18
19	20	21	22	23	24	25
26	27	28	29	30	31	

November
S	M	T	W	T	F	S
						1
2	3	4	5	6	7	8
9	10	11	12	13	14	15
16	17	18	19	20	21	22
23	24	25	26	27	28	29
30						

December
S	M	T	W	T	F	S
	1	2	3	4	5	6
7	8	9	10	11	12	13
14	15	16	17	18	19	20
21	22	23	24	25	26	27
28	29	30	31			

The Left-Hander's 2025 Calendar by Cary Koegle
copyright © 2024 by Charles Koegle and Donald Koegle. Printed in China. No part of this calendar may be used or reproduced in any manner whatsoever without written permission except in the case of reprints in the context of reviews. For information write Andrews McMeel Publishing, a division of Andrews McMeel Universal, 1130 Walnut Street, Kansas City, Missouri 64106.

This edition published by arrangement with Price Stern Sloan, an imprint of Penguin Young Readers Group, a division of Penguin Random House LLC.

Phases of the moon and start dates for the seasons of the year are presented in Universal Time.

Every effort has been made to ensure the accuracy of listed holiday dates; however, some may have changed after publication for official or cultural reasons.

www.andrewsmcmeel.com

ISBN: 978-1-5248-8990-6

Follow our sustainability journey at publishing.andrewsmcmeel.com/sustainability.

ARE YOU LEFT-HANDED?

Ten activities for hand-preference testing include: writing, drawing, eating with a spoon, cutting with a knife, throwing a ball, brushing one's teeth, striking a match, opening a jar or box, holding a broom, and using scissors. If you perform all these tasks with your left hand, you are considered a "strong left-hander." That percentage is much smaller than those who perform half or more and are still considered a lefty.

		December 2024				
S	M	T	W	T	F	S
1	2	3	4	5	6	7
8	9	10	11	12	13	14
15	16	17	18	19	20	21
22	23	24	25	26	27	28
29	30	31				

		January 2025				
S	M	T	W	T	F	S
			1	2	3	4
5	6	7	8	9	10	11
12	13	14	15	16	17	18
19	20	21	22	23	24	25
26	27	28	29	30	31	

DEC '24–JAN '25

MONDAY
30
● New Moon

TUESDAY
31

WEDNESDAY
1
New Year's Day
Kwanzaa ends
Lefty birthday: Actor Frank Langella

THURSDAY
2
Hanukkah ends at sundown
Lefty birthday: Actress Renée Elise Goldsberry

FRIDAY
3
Lefty birthday: Hockey player Bobby Hull

SATURDAY
4
Lefty birthday: Physicist Sir Isaac Newton

SUNDAY
5
Lefty birthday: Musician Elizabeth Cotten

LEFTIES PLAYING LEFTIES

Judy Davis played fellow southpaw songbird Judy Garland in the biopic *Life with Judy Garland: Me and My Shadows.* Davis won a Primetime Emmy Award for Outstanding Lead Actress in a Miniseries or a Movie for her role.

			January 2025			
S	M	T	W	T	F	S
				1	2	3	4
5	6	7	8	9	10	11
12	13	14	15	16	17	18
19	20	21	22	23	24	25
26	27	28	29	30	31	

JANUARY

MONDAY

6

☽ First Quarter
Lefty birthday: Joan of Arc

TUESDAY

7

Lefty birthday: Actor Jeremy Renner

WEDNESDAY

8

Lefty birthday: Musician David Bowie

THURSDAY

9

Lefty birthday: Singer Crystal Gayle

FRIDAY

10

Lefty birthday: Baseball player Willie McCovey

SATURDAY

11

Lefty birthday: Former secretary of the treasury Alexander Hamilton

SUNDAY

12

Lefty birthday: Boxer Joe Frazier

Even though he died in 2022, Pelé is still widely regarded as one of the best players of all time and appeared on twenty-six "Greatest" lists in 2023. This lefty soccer player was named Athlete of the Century by the International Olympic Committee in 1999 and was included in the "*Time* 100" list of the most important people of the twentieth century. In 2000, Pelé was voted World Player of the Century. His record of 1,279 goals in 1,363 games is recognized as a Guinness World Record. A global star, Pelé was declared a national treasure in his native Brazil.

January 2025

S	M	T	W	T	F	S
			1	2	3	4
5	6	7	8	9	10	11
12	13	14	15	16	17	18
19	20	21	22	23	24	25
26	27	28	29	30	31	

JANUARY

MONDAY
13
○ **Full Moon**
Lefty birthday: Actress Penelope Ann Miller

TUESDAY
14
Lefty birthday: Doctor and missionary Albert Schweitzer

WEDNESDAY
15
Lefty birthday: Civil rights activist Martin Luther King Jr.

THURSDAY
16
Lefty birthday: Guitarist Barbara Lynn

FRIDAY
17
Lefty birthday: Inventor and philosopher Benjamin Franklin

SATURDAY
18
Lefty birthday: Comedian Danny Kaye

SUNDAY
19
Lefty birthday: Politician Pete Buttigieg

INSPIRATION FROM LEFTIES

Injustice anywhere is a threat to justice everywhere.

—Martin Luther King Jr.

January 2025

S	M	T	W	T	F	S
			1	2	3	4
5	6	7	8	9	10	11
12	13	14	15	16	17	18
19	20	21	22	23	24	25
26	27	28	29	30	31	

JANUARY

MONDAY

20

Martin Luther King Jr. Day
Lefty birthday: Comedian George Burns

TUESDAY

21

◑ Last Quarter
Lefty birthday: Tennis player Laura Robson

WEDNESDAY

22

Lefty birthday: Actress Diane Lane

THURSDAY

23

Lefty birthday: Tennis player Petr Korda

FRIDAY

24

Lefty birthday: Comedienne Kristen Schaal

SATURDAY

25

Lefty birthday: Singer Alicia Keys

SUNDAY

26

Lefty birthday: Actor Scott Glenn

LEFTY OR NOT?

Mayim Bialik was born in San Diego and, as a child actress, appeared in numerous television series, eventually landing her long-running role in *Blossom*. Aside from acting, Bialik earned a bachelor of science degree in neuroscience with minors in Hebrew and Jewish studies from UCLA and a PhD in neuroscience from UCLA in 2007. When asked whether she was left-handed, Bialik replied, "I am mixed-handed. I was born a righty. My mother was a lefty. My brother was a lefty. I was in a significant car accident eight years ago, which made me have to become much more ambidextrous. So, I actually do all sports lefty. So, yeah. I guess I'm mixed-handed but mostly right."

January 2025

S	M	T	W	T	F	S
			1	2	3	4
5	6	7	8	9	10	11
12	13	14	15	16	17	18
19	20	21	22	23	24	25
26	27	28	29	30	31	

February 2025

S	M	T	W	T	F	S
						1
2	3	4	5	6	7	8
9	10	11	12	13	14	15
16	17	18	19	20	21	22
23	24	25	26	27	28	

JAN-FEB

MONDAY
27
Lefty birthday: Author Lewis Carroll

TUESDAY
28
Lefty birthday: Physicist Auguste Piccard

WEDNESDAY
29
● New Moon
Lefty birthday: Talk show host Oprah Winfrey

THURSDAY
30
Lefty birthday: Singer Phil Collins

FRIDAY
31

SATURDAY
1
Lefty birthday: Martial artist and actress Ronda Rousey

SUNDAY
2
Lefty birthday: Actor Brent Spiner

Considered the greatest German literary figure of the modern era, influential lefty Johann Wolfgang von Goethe was a German writer, poet, novelist, playwright, natural philosopher, and scientist. He was born in 1749 and is probably best known for *The Sorrows of Young Werther,* the first novel of the Sturm und Drang movement, and for his dramatic work *Faust,* which he wrote over a period of fifty years. Goethe also wrote treatises on botany, anatomy, and color. There are more than ten thousand letters and nearly three thousand drawings by him that have survived.

February 2025

S	M	T	W	T	F	S
						1
2	3	4	5	6	7	8
9	10	11	12	13	14	15
16	17	18	19	20	21	22
23	24	25	26	27	28	

FEBRUARY

MONDAY

3

Lefty birthday: Baseball player Fred Lynn

TUESDAY

4

Lefty birthday: Boxer Oscar De La Hoya

WEDNESDAY

5

◑ First Quarter
Lefty birthday: Actor Abhishek Bachchan

THURSDAY

6

Lefty birthday: Former president Ronald Reagan

FRIDAY

7

Lefty birthday: Painter and writer Henry Fuseli

SATURDAY

8

Lefty birthday: Journalist Ted Koppel

SUNDAY

9

Lefty birthday: Baseball player John Kruk

LEFTY LOVEBIRDS

Emperor Napoleon Bonaparte and Empress Joséphine de Beauharnais

Matthew Broderick and Sarah Jessica Parker

Joel Coen and Frances McDormand

Pierre Curie and Marie Curie

Frédéric Joliot-Curie and Irène Joliot-Curie

February 2025

S	M	T	W	T	F	S
						1
2	3	4	5	6	7	8
9	10	11	12	13	14	15
16	17	18	19	20	21	22
23	24	25	26	27	28	

FEBRUARY

MONDAY

10

Lefty birthday: Olympic gold medalist Mark Spitz

TUESDAY

11

Lefty birthday: Inventor Thomas Edison

WEDNESDAY

12

○ Full Moon
Lefty birthday: Basketball player Bill Russell

THURSDAY

13

Lefty birthday: Actress Kim Novak

FRIDAY

14

Valentine's Day
Lefty birthday: Politician Michael Bloomberg

SATURDAY

15

Lefty birthday: Cartoonist Matt Groening

SUNDAY

16

Lefty birthday: Tennis player John McEnroe

NAME THE LEFTIES

Q: What three U.S. president and vice-president teams were both left-handed?

A: Gerald Ford and Nelson Rockefeller
Ronald Reagan and George H. W. Bush
Bill Clinton and Al Gore

February 2025

S	M	T	W	T	F	S
						1
2	3	4	5	6	7	8
9	10	11	12	13	14	15
16	17	18	19	20	21	22
23	24	25	26	27	28	

FEBRUARY

MONDAY

17

Presidents' Day
Lefty birthday: Actor Richard Karn

TUESDAY

18

Lefty birthday: Baseball player Ila Borders

WEDNESDAY

19

Lefty birthday: Guitarist Tony Iommi

THURSDAY

20

☽ Last Quarter
Lefty birthday: Musician Kurt Cobain

FRIDAY

21

Lefty birthday: Actress Mélanie Laurent

SATURDAY

22

Lefty birthday: Boy Scouts founder Robert Baden-Powell

SUNDAY

23

Lefty birthday: Guitarist Johnny Winter

INSPIRATION FROM LEFTIES

When you make the right decision, it doesn't really matter what anyone else thinks.

—Caroline Kennedy

FEB-MAR

MONDAY
24
Lefty birthday: Cricket player Brian Close

TUESDAY
25
Lefty birthday: Opera singer Enrico Caruso

WEDNESDAY
26
Lefty birthday: Politician Tim Kaine

THURSDAY
27
Lefty birthday: Actress Joanne Woodward

FRIDAY
28
● New Moon
Ramadan
Lefty birthday: Scientist Linus Pauling

SATURDAY
1
Lefty birthday: Singer Justin Bieber

SUNDAY
2
Lefty birthday: Football player Sebastian Janikowski

Designer Shea McGee grew up in Texas and moved to Utah to attend Brigham Young University, where she met her future husband, Syd. This left-hander started documenting her Southern California studio apartment renovations on social media in 2013, and that led to the creation of a furniture and decor business, McGee & Co. When the couple moved back to Utah, they once again turned to social media and documented the renovation of their home, and Studio McGee was born. In their first six years in business, the couple was featured in *Architectural Digest, Domino, House Beautiful,* and *Vogue Living.*

March 2025

S	M	T	W	T	F	S
						1
2	3	4	5	6	7	8
9	10	11	12	13	14	15
16	17	18	19	20	21	22
23	24	25	26	27	28	29
30	31					

MARCH

MONDAY

3

Lefty birthday: Cartoonist Ronald Searle

TUESDAY

4

Lefty birthday: Baseball player Francis "Lefty" O'Doul

WEDNESDAY

5

Ash Wednesday
Lefty birthday: Actor Sir Rex Harrison

THURSDAY

6

◐ First Quarter
Lefty birthday: Artist Michelangelo

FRIDAY

7

Lefty birthday: Composer Maurice Ravel

SATURDAY

8

Lefty birthday: Tennis player Petra Kvitová

SUNDAY

9

Daylight Saving Time begins
Lefty birthday: Wrestler Nikita Koloff

CHARITABLE LEFTY

Lefty entrepreneur Richard Branson started his first charity, Student Valley Centre, when he was only seventeen. He now supports many causes, including gender equality, LGBTQ rights, environmental conservation, and climate change. The first person to ride into space aboard his own spacecraft, Branson has also funded educational charities in Africa; formed The Elders, a group of global leaders working objectively to solve difficult global conflicts; established his nonprofit Virgin Unite to bring entrepreneurs and philanthropists together to solve global problems; and pledged to give away half of his fortune to charity.

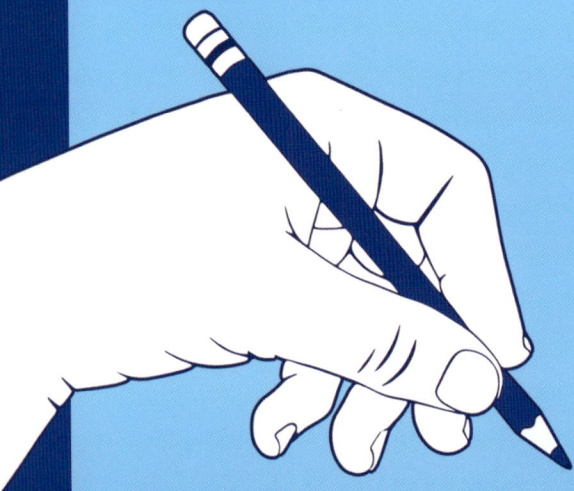

March 2025

S	M	T	W	T	F	S
						1
2	3	4	5	6	7	8
9	10	11	12	13	14	15
16	17	18	19	20	21	22
23	24	25	26	27	28	29
30	31					

MARCH

MONDAY
10
Commonwealth Day (Canada)
Lefty birthday: Lefthanders International founder Dean R. Campbell

TUESDAY
11
Lefty birthday: Actor Peter Berg

WEDNESDAY
12
Lefty birthday: Astronaut Wally Schirra

THURSDAY
13
Purim begins at sundown
Lefty birthday: Baseball player Will Clark

FRIDAY
14
○ Full Moon
Lefty birthday: Physicist Albert Einstein

SATURDAY
15
Lefty birthday: Former Supreme Court justice Ruth Bader Ginsburg

SUNDAY
16
Lefty birthday: Comic artist Todd McFarlane

Did you know that when southpaw Nicole Kidman portrayed right-handed Virginia Woolf in the film *The Hours,* she learned to write with her right hand? She said, "I learned to write with my right hand for it. People look at me, like, that's crazy, and I'm like, no, it was necessary." Her authenticity and lack of a hand double culminated in numerous accolades, including an Academy Award.

March 2025

S	M	T	W	T	F	S
						1
2	3	4	5	6	7	8
9	10	11	12	13	14	15
16	17	18	19	20	21	22
23	24	25	26	27	28	29
30	31					

MARCH

MONDAY
17
St. Patrick's Day

TUESDAY
18
Lefty birthday: Former South African president Frederik Willem de Klerk

WEDNESDAY
19
Lefty birthday: Actor Bruce Willis

THURSDAY
20
Vernal Equinox
Lefty birthday: Formula One racer Ayrton Senna

FRIDAY
21

SATURDAY
22
◐ Last Quarter
Lefty birthday: Tennis player Ilana Kloss

SUNDAY
23
Lefty birthday: Actress Michelle Monaghan

INSPIRATION FROM LEFTIES

Every action needs to be prompted by a motive.

—Leonardo da Vinci

March 2025

S	M	T	W	T	F	S
						1
2	3	4	5	6	7	8
9	10	11	12	13	14	15
16	17	18	19	20	21	22
23	24	25	26	27	28	29
30	31					

MARCH

MONDAY
24
Lefty birthday: Fashion entrepreneur Tommy Hilfiger

TUESDAY
25
Lefty birthday: Bowler Mike Aulby

WEDNESDAY
26
Lefty birthday: Actor James Caan

THURSDAY
27
Lefty birthday: King Louis XVII of France

FRIDAY
28
Lefty birthday: Singer Lady Gaga

SATURDAY
29
● New Moon
Lefty birthday: Baseball player Eric Gunderson

SUNDAY
30
Eid al-Fitr
Lefty birthday: Singer Céline Dion

Born and raised in Louisville, Kentucky, Jennifer Lawrence graduated from high school early in order to start her acting career at age fourteen. Her breakout performance in *Winter's Bone* earned Lawrence an Academy Award nomination for Best Actress. At age twenty, this lefty was the second-youngest actress ever to be nominated for this award. She went on to win the Oscar for her role in *Silver Linings Playbook,* becoming the second-youngest winner at twenty-two. Her other notable films include *X-Men: First Class,* the Hunger Games series, *American Hustle, Red Sparrow, Don't Look Up,* and *No Hard Feelings.* Lawrence is a feminist who advocates for women's reproductive rights. In 2015, she founded the Jennifer Lawrence Foundation, which advocates for the Boys & Girls Clubs of America and the Special Olympics.

March 2025

S	M	T	W	T	F	S
						1
2	3	4	5	6	7	8
9	10	11	12	13	14	15
16	17	18	19	20	21	22
23	24	25	26	27	28	29
30	31					

April 2025

S	M	T	W	T	F	S
		1	2	3	4	5
6	7	8	9	10	11	12
13	14	15	16	17	18	19
20	21	22	23	24	25	26
27	28	29	30			

MAR–APR

MONDAY

31

Lefty birthday: Former vice president Al Gore

TUESDAY

1

Lefty birthday: Composer Sergei Rachmaninoff

WEDNESDAY

2

Lefty birthday: Emperor Charlemagne

THURSDAY

3

Lefty birthday: Actress Marsha Mason

FRIDAY

4

Lefty birthday: Actor Anthony Perkins

SATURDAY

5

◐ First Quarter
Lefty birthday: Former secretary of state Colin Powell

SUNDAY

6

Lefty birthday: Painter Raphael

According to ranker.com, the top ten lefty athletes of all time as of 2023 were:

Pelé

Babe Ruth

Bill Russell

Wayne Gretzky

Larry Bird

Rafael Nadal

LeBron James

Ted Williams

John McEnroe

Deion Sanders

April 2025

S	M	T	W	T	F	S
		1	2	3	4	5
6	7	8	9	10	11	12
13	14	15	16	17	18	19
20	21	22	23	24	25	26
27	28	29	30			

APRIL

MONDAY

7

Lefty birthday: Singer John Oates

TUESDAY

8

Lefty birthday: Musician Glen Burtnik

WEDNESDAY

9

Lefty birthday: Actor Dennis Quaid

THURSDAY

10

Lefty birthday: Musician Babyface

FRIDAY

11

Lefty birthday: Model Alessandra Ambrosio

SATURDAY

12

Passover begins at sundown
Lefty birthday: Singer Tiny Tim

SUNDAY

13

○ **Full Moon**
Palm Sunday
Lefty birthday: Author Eudora Welty

INSPIRATION FROM LEFTIES

Hope is being able to see that there is light despite all of the darkness.

—Desmond Tutu

April 2025

S	M	T	W	T	F	S
		1	2	3	4	5
6	7	8	9	10	11	12
13	14	15	16	17	18	19
20	21	22	23	24	25	26
27	28	29	30			

APRIL

MONDAY

14

Lefty birthday: Actor Rod Steiger

TUESDAY

15

Lefty birthday: Artist and scientist Leonardo da Vinci

WEDNESDAY

16

Lefty birthday: Actor Sir Charlie Chaplin

THURSDAY

17

Lefty birthday: Football player Norman "Boomer" Esiason

FRIDAY

18

Good Friday (Western)
Holy Friday (Orthodox)
Lefty birthday: Lawyer Clarence Darrow

SATURDAY

19

Lefty birthday: Actress Kate Hudson

SUNDAY

20

Easter (Western, Orthodox)
Passover ends at sundown
Lefty birthday: Baseball player Don Mattingly

THE QUOTABLE LEFTY

While right-handed people rarely think about which hand another person is using, lefties are quick to spot a fellow southpaw. We've been watching other members of our exclusive club since the beginning of recorded history.

—Rae Lindsay, *Left Is Right: The Survival Guide for Living Lefty in a Right-Handed World*

April 2025

S	M	T	W	T	F	S
		1	2	3	4	5
6	7	8	9	10	11	12
13	14	15	16	17	18	19
20	21	22	23	24	25	26
27	28	29	30			

APRIL

MONDAY
21
◐ Last Quarter
Easter Monday (Canada)
Lefty birthday: Musician Iggy Pop

TUESDAY
22
Lefty birthday: Golfer Eric Axley

WEDNESDAY
23
Yom HaShoah begins at sundown
Lefty birthday: Criminologist Alphonse Bertillon

THURSDAY
24
Lefty birthday: Actress Shirley MacLaine

FRIDAY
25
Lefty birthday: Journalist Edward R. Murrow

SATURDAY
26
Lefty birthday: Comedienne Carol Burnett

SUNDAY
27
● New Moon
Lefty birthday: Bowler Earl Anthony

Left-handers comprise approximately 15 percent of professional tennis players but only 11 percent of the general population. In boxing, baseball, fencing, table tennis, and specialist batting positions in cricket, the contrast is even starker, with 30 percent or more of top players often being left-handed.

April 2025

S	M	T	W	T	F	S
		1	2	3	4	5
6	7	8	9	10	11	12
13	14	15	16	17	18	19
20	21	22	23	24	25	26
27	28	29	30			

May 2025

S	M	T	W	T	F	S
				1	2	3
4	5	6	7	8	9	10
11	12	13	14	15	16	17
18	19	20	21	22	23	24
25	26	27	28	29	30	31

APR-MAY

MONDAY
28
Lefty birthday: Actress Jessica Alba

TUESDAY
29
Lefty birthday: Comedian Jerry Seinfeld

WEDNESDAY
30
Lefty birthday: Cartoonist Barry Blitt

THURSDAY
1
Lefty birthday: Cartoonist Bob Mankoff

FRIDAY
2
Lefty birthday: Olympic gold medalist Sarah Hughes

SATURDAY
3
Lefty birthday: Singer Frankie Valli

SUNDAY
4
◐ First Quarter
Lefty birthday: Musician Dick Dale

MOTHER AND CHILD LEFTIES

Marie Curie and Irène Joliot-Curie

Goldie Hawn and Kate Hudson

Anne Meara and Ben Stiller

May 2025

S	M	T	W	T	F	S
				1	2	3
4	5	6	7	8	9	10
11	12	13	14	15	16	17
18	19	20	21	22	23	24
25	26	27	28	29	30	31

MAY

MONDAY

5

Lefty birthday: Basketball player Harold Miner

TUESDAY

6

Lefty birthday: Musician John Flansburgh

WEDNESDAY

7

Lefty birthday: Actor and director Philip Charles MacKenzie

THURSDAY

8

Lefty birthday: Former president Harry S. Truman

FRIDAY

9

Lefty birthday: Golfer Sam Adams

SATURDAY

10

Lefty birthday: Dancer Fred Astaire

SUNDAY

11

Mother's Day
Lefty birthday: Football player Matt Leinart

INSPIRATION FROM LEFTIES

Some people look like they're lost causes, but they're not. Even if they're in a messed-up situation, the one little thing you do to help can go a long way.

—LaKeith Stanfield

May 2025

S	M	T	W	T	F	S
				1	2	3
4	5	6	7	8	9	10
11	12	13	14	15	16	17
18	19	20	21	22	23	24
25	26	27	28	29	30	31

MAY

MONDAY

12

○ Full Moon
Lefty birthday: Baseball player Yogi Berra

TUESDAY

13

Lefty birthday: Author Armistead Maupin

WEDNESDAY

14

Lefty birthday: Singer David Byrne

THURSDAY

15

Lefty birthday: Scientist Pierre Curie

FRIDAY

16

Lefty birthday: Musician Robert Fripp

SATURDAY

17

Armed Forces Day
Lefty birthday: Singer and songwriter Jordan Knight

SUNDAY

18

Lefty birthday: Actress Tina Fey

Southpaw pitcher for the Atlanta Braves and NY Mets, Tom Glavine was born in Massachusetts and played baseball and hockey in high school. Even though he was drafted by the Los Angeles Kings, Glavine chose baseball. A two-time Cy Young Award winner, he was MVP of the 1995 World Series for the Braves and was elected to the Baseball Hall of Fame in 2014, his first year of eligibility.

May 2025

S	M	T	W	T	F	S
				1	2	3
4	5	6	7	8	9	10
11	12	13	14	15	16	17
18	19	20	21	22	23	24
25	26	27	28	29	30	31

MAY

MONDAY

19

Victoria Day (Canada)

TUESDAY

20

◐ Last Quarter
Lefty birthday: Baseball player David Wells

WEDNESDAY

21

Lefty birthday: Painter Albrecht Dürer

THURSDAY

22

Lefty birthday: Conductor Peter Nero

FRIDAY

23

Lefty birthday: Jeopardy! winner Ken Jennings

SATURDAY

24

Lefty birthday: Singer-songwriter Bob Dylan

SUNDAY

25

Lefty birthday: Actress Karen Valentine

NAME THE LEFTY

Q: Left-handers Penelope Ann Miller and Anne Meara appeared in the Oscar-nominated 1990 film *Awakenings*. The star of that film was also a lefty. Can you name him?

A: Robert De Niro

May 2025						
S	M	T	W	T	F	S
				1	2	3
4	5	6	7	8	9	10
11	12	13	14	15	16	17
18	19	20	21	22	23	24
25	26	27	28	29	30	31

June 2025						
S	M	T	W	T	F	S
1	2	3	4	5	6	7
8	9	10	11	12	13	14
15	16	17	18	19	20	21
22	23	24	25	26	27	28
29	30					

MAY-JUN

MONDAY
26
Memorial Day
Lefty birthday: Singer Lauryn Hill

TUESDAY
27
● New Moon
Lefty birthday: Lawman James "Wild Bill" Hickok

WEDNESDAY
28
Lefty birthday: Actress and quintuplet Marie Dionne

THURSDAY
29
Lefty birthday: Musician Noel Gallagher

FRIDAY
30
Lefty birthday: Football player Gale Sayers

SATURDAY
31
Lefty birthday: Actor Denholm Elliott

SUNDAY
1
Shavuot begins at sundown
Lefty birthday: Actress Marilyn Monroe

NAME THE LEFTY

Q: Lefty actress and model Angie Harmon and her husband delivered a speech at the 2004 Republican National Convention. The candidate they were supporting was also a lefty. Can you name him?

A: John McCain

June 2025

S	M	T	W	T	F	S
1	2	3	4	5	6	7
8	9	10	11	12	13	14
15	16	17	18	19	20	21
22	23	24	25	26	27	28
29	30					

JUNE

MONDAY

2

Lefty birthday: Baseball player Raúl Ibañez

TUESDAY

3

◐ First Quarter
Shavuot ends at sundown
Lefty birthday: Painter Raoul Dufy

WEDNESDAY

4

Lefty birthday: Actress Angelina Jolie

THURSDAY

5

Lefty birthday: Actor Mark Wahlberg

FRIDAY

6

Eid al-Adha
Lefty birthday: Baseball player Bill Dickey

SATURDAY

7

Lefty birthday: Musician Prince

SUNDAY

8

Lefty birthday: Bowler Tish Johnson

SPORTY FATHER AND SON LEFTIES

Fencers Giuseppe and Edoardo Mangiarotti

Golfers Russ Cochran and Ryan Cochran-Siegle

Hockey players Bobby and Brett Hull

June 2025

S	M	T	W	T	F	S
1	2	3	4	5	6	7
8	9	10	11	12	13	14
15	16	17	18	19	20	21
22	23	24	25	26	27	28
29	30					

JUNE

MONDAY

9

Lefty birthday: Composer Cole Porter

TUESDAY

10

Lefty birthday: Actress Judy Garland

WEDNESDAY

11

○ Full Moon
Lefty birthday: Musician Graham Russell

THURSDAY

12

Lefty birthday: Former president George H. W. Bush

FRIDAY

13

Lefty birthday: Actor Tim Allen

SATURDAY

14

Flag Day

SUNDAY

15

Father's Day
Lefty birthday: Jazz musician Erroll Garner

INSPIRATION FROM LEFTIES

Your ordinary acts of love and hope point to the extraordinary promise that every human life is of inestimable value.

—Desmond Tutu

June 2025

S	M	T	W	T	F	S
1	2	3	4	5	6	7
8	9	10	11	12	13	14
15	16	17	18	19	20	21
22	23	24	25	26	27	28
29	30					

JUNE

MONDAY

16

Lefty birthday: Baseball player Wally Joyner

TUESDAY

17

Lefty birthday: Artist M. C. Escher

WEDNESDAY

18

◗ Last Quarter
Lefty birthday: Singer-songwriter Sir Paul McCartney

THURSDAY

19

Juneteenth
Lefty birthday: Baseball player Lou Gehrig

FRIDAY

20

Lefty birthday: Actress Nicole Kidman

SATURDAY

21

Summer Solstice
National Indigenous Peoples Day (Canada)
Lefty birthday: William, Prince of Wales

SUNDAY

22

Lefty birthday: Baseball player Carl Hubbell

THE LEFT STUFF

As Gear Patrol states, "Lefties are rare . . . but left-handed watches are even rarer." That's why they've collected several left-handed watches for southpaws. They have crowns located at nine o'clock instead of the usual three o'clock. Check them out at gearpatrol.com.

June 2025

S	M	T	W	T	F	S
1	2	3	4	5	6	7
8	9	10	11	12	13	14
15	16	17	18	19	20	21
22	23	24	25	26	27	28
29	30					

JUNE

MONDAY
23
Lefty birthday: Mathematician Alan Turing

TUESDAY
24
Lefty birthday: Hockey player Wayne Cashman

WEDNESDAY
25
● New Moon
Lefty birthday: Singer Carly Simon

THURSDAY
26
Lefty birthday: Singer Chris Isaak

FRIDAY
27
Lefty birthday: Author and educator Helen Keller

SATURDAY
28
Lefty birthday: Actress Mary Stuart Masterson

SUNDAY
29
Lefty birthday: Drummer Ian Paice

Born Robert Zimmerman in Hibbing, Minnesota, Bob Dylan is a singer-songwriter, musician, poet, film director, and painter. Many of this lefty's early songs became anthems for the civil rights and peace movements, and he is considered one of the most influential figures both musically and culturally. Dylan was included in "*Time* 100: The Most Important People of the Century," in which he was called "master poet, caustic social critic and intrepid, guiding spirit of the counterculture generation." His numerous awards include the Presidential Medal of Freedom, ten Grammy Awards, a Golden Globe Award, and an Academy Award. He has been inducted into the Rock and Roll Hall of Fame, the Nashville Songwriters Hall of Fame, and the Songwriters Hall of Fame. In 2016, Dylan was awarded the Nobel Prize in Literature "for having created new poetic expressions within the great American song tradition."

June 2025

S	M	T	W	T	F	S
1	2	3	4	5	6	7
8	9	10	11	12	13	14
15	16	17	18	19	20	21
22	23	24	25	26	27	28
29	30					

July 2025

S	M	T	W	T	F	S
		1	2	3	4	5
6	7	8	9	10	11	12
13	14	15	16	17	18	19
20	21	22	23	24	25	26
27	28	29	30	31		

JUN–JUL

MONDAY

30

Lefty birthday: Oceanographer Robert D. Ballard

TUESDAY

1

Canada Day
Lefty birthday: Actor Dan Aykroyd

WEDNESDAY

2

☽ First Quarter
Lefty birthday: Baseball player Joe Magrane

THURSDAY

3

Lefty birthday: Humorist Dave Barry

FRIDAY

4

Independence Day

SATURDAY

5

Lefty birthday: Founder of the Davis Cup Dwight Davis

SUNDAY

6

Lefty birthday: Actor Sylvester Stallone

Seventy-four percent of left-handers claim to be left-eye dominant. To determine your eye dominance, make a triangle with your hands and center an object within the triangle. Now close one eye. Then change eyes. When the object stays reasonably centered within the triangle, that is your dominant eye.

			July 2025			
S	M	T	W	T	F	S
		1	2	3	4	5
6	7	8	9	10	11	12
13	14	15	16	17	18	19
20	21	22	23	24	25	26
27	28	29	30	31		

JULY

MONDAY

7

Lefty birthday: Musician Sir Ringo Starr

TUESDAY

8

Lefty birthday: Former vice president Nelson Rockefeller

WEDNESDAY

9

Lefty birthday: Inventor Elias Howe

THURSDAY

10

○ **Full Moon**
Lefty birthday: Inventor Nikola Tesla

FRIDAY

11

Lefty birthday: Soccer player Hugo Sánchez

SATURDAY

12

Lefty birthday: Actress Alison Wright

SUNDAY

13

Lefty birthday: Chef Paul Prudhomme

INSPIRATION FROM LEFTIES

No matter what you're doing, live it. Make an experience. Have fun. Relate to someone. Take them in. Learn.

—Minka Kelly

July 2025

S	M	T	W	T	F	S
		1	2	3	4	5
6	7	8	9	10	11	12
13	14	15	16	17	18	19
20	21	22	23	24	25	26
27	28	29	30	31		

JULY

MONDAY

14

Lefty birthday: Former president Gerald Ford

TUESDAY

15

Lefty birthday: Painter Rembrandt

WEDNESDAY

16

Lefty birthday: Baseball player "Shoeless" Joe Jackson

THURSDAY

17

FRIDAY

18

◐ Last Quarter
Lefty birthday: Entrepreneur Sir Richard Branson

SATURDAY

19

Lefty birthday: Singer Vikki Carr

SUNDAY

20

Lefty birthday: World leader Alexander the Great

Left-handed medical humanitarian Paul Farmer created specific drug-therapy initiatives for individuals in Haiti, Peru, and Russia. This aided global multi-drug-resistant tuberculosis treatment programs, ensuring successful delivery of antibiotics. That cause was helped by a $44.7 million grant from the fellow lefty Bill Gates through the Bill & Melinda Gates Foundation.

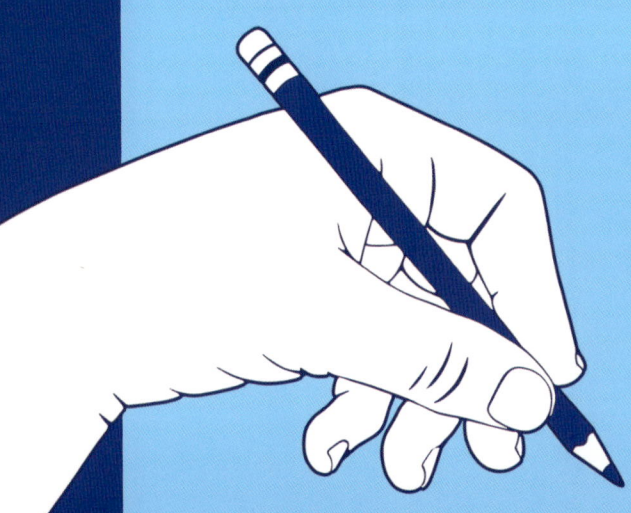

July 2025

S	M	T	W	T	F	S
		1	2	3	4	5
6	7	8	9	10	11	12
13	14	15	16	17	18	19
20	21	22	23	24	25	26
27	28	29	30	31		

JULY

MONDAY
21
Lefty birthday: Author and philosopher Marshall McLuhan

TUESDAY
22
Lefty birthday: Comedian David Spade

WEDNESDAY
23
Lefty birthday: Former Supreme Court justice Anthony Kennedy

THURSDAY
24
● New Moon
Lefty birthday: Political cartoonist Pat Oliphant

FRIDAY
25
Lefty birthday: Actress Barbara Harris

SATURDAY
26
Lefty birthday: Olympic gold medalist Dorothy Hamill

SUNDAY
27
Lefty birthday: Cricket player Allan Border

LEFTY OR NOT?

When former University of Alabama quarterback Tua Tagovailoa threw the game-winning pass in the 2017 college football national championship, he did it with his left arm. Even though he prefers his right hand for everything else, this current Miami Dolphins player is considered the NFL's only left-handed starting quarterback.

July 2025

S	M	T	W	T	F	S
		1	2	3	4	5
6	7	8	9	10	11	12
13	14	15	16	17	18	19
20	21	22	23	24	25	26
27	28	29	30	31		

August 2025

S	M	T	W	T	F	S
					1	2
3	4	5	6	7	8	9
10	11	12	13	14	15	16
17	18	19	20	21	22	23
24	25	26	27	28	29	30
31						

JUL-AUG

MONDAY

28

Lefty birthday: Basketball player and politician Bill Bradley

TUESDAY

29

Lefty birthday: Singer Martina McBride

WEDNESDAY

30

Lefty birthday: Automobile inventor Henry Ford

THURSDAY

31

Lefty birthday: Actor Barry Van Dyke

FRIDAY

1

◐ First Quarter
Lefty birthday: Baseball player Madison Bumgarner

SATURDAY

2

Lefty birthday: Writer James Baldwin

SUNDAY

3

Lefty birthday: Architect Jan des Bouvrie

ROYAL LEFTIES

King Charles III of the United Kingdom, the longest-waiting heir in British history, became king on September 8, 2022. This lefty is also the oldest person to accede to the British throne. His coronation took place at Westminster Abbey on May 6, 2023. The new heir apparent, William, Prince of Wales, is also left-handed, like his father.

August 2025

S	M	T	W	T	F	S
					1	2
3	4	5	6	7	8	9
10	11	12	13	14	15	16
17	18	19	20	21	22	23
24	25	26	27	28	29	30
31						

AUGUST

MONDAY

4

Civic Day (Canada)
Lefty birthday: Former president Barack Obama

TUESDAY

5

Lefty birthday: Baseball player John Olerud

WEDNESDAY

6

Lefty birthday: Bacteriologist Sir Alexander Fleming

THURSDAY

7

Lefty birthday: Actor David Duchovny

FRIDAY

8

Lefty birthday: Actor Keith Carradine

SATURDAY

9

○ **Full Moon**
Lefty birthday: Tennis player Rod Laver

SUNDAY

10

Lefty birthday: Former president Herbert Hoover

August 13 is International Left-Handers Day. Launched in 1992, this yearly event celebrates left-handedness and raises awareness of the difficulties and frustrations left-handers experience every day in a world designed for right-handers.

August 2025						
S	M	T	W	T	F	S
					1	2
3	4	5	6	7	8	9
10	11	12	13	14	15	16
17	18	19	20	21	22	23
24	25	26	27	28	29	30
31						

AUGUST

MONDAY
11
Lefty birthday: Boxer Jack Bodell

TUESDAY
12
Lefty birthday: Musician Mark Knopfler

WEDNESDAY
13
International Left-Handers Day
Lefty birthday: Golfer Ben Hogan

THURSDAY
14
Lefty birthday: Football player Tim Tebow

FRIDAY
15
Lefty birthday: Emperor Napoléon Bonaparte

SATURDAY
16
◐ Last Quarter
Lefty birthday: Director James Cameron

SUNDAY
17
Lefty birthday: Tennis player Guillermo Vilas

INSPIRATION FROM LEFTIES

If you can't convince 'em, confuse 'em.

—Harry S. Truman

August 2025

S	M	T	W	T	F	S
					1	2
3	4	5	6	7	8	9
10	11	12	13	14	15	16
17	18	19	20	21	22	23
24	25	26	27	28	29	30
31						

AUGUST

MONDAY
18
Lefty birthday: Actor and director Robert Redford

TUESDAY
19
Lefty birthday: Former president Bill Clinton

WEDNESDAY
20
Lefty birthday: Singer Robert Plant

THURSDAY
21
Lefty birthday: Musician Joe Strummer

FRIDAY
22
Lefty birthday: General H. Norman Schwarzkopf Jr.

SATURDAY
23
● New Moon
Lefty birthday: King Louis XVI of France

SUNDAY
24
Lefty birthday: Actress Marlee Matlin

Malina Moye is a singer-songwriter, lefty guitarist, model, actress, and entrepreneur. Often compared to fellow left-handers Jimi Hendrix and Eric Gales, Moye is known for her fusion of a variety of different genres, including rock, blues, funk, and soul. She plays left-handed but strings her guitars upside down. Moye founded WCE Records in 2004, has released four studio albums, performed for the queen of England, and was the first African American woman to play the National Anthem on electric guitar at a professional sporting event. In 2020, her single "Enough" had a resurgence with the Black Lives Matter movement, and in 2021, the Rock and Roll Hall of Fame chose to feature Moye as one of today's most influential artists. In 2021, music company Dean Markley announced the release of the Malina Moye Signature Guitar Strings, making her the first woman of color in history to have her own line of strings.

August 2025

S	M	T	W	T	F	S
					1	2
3	4	5	6	7	8	9
10	11	12	13	14	15	16
17	18	19	20	21	22	23
24	25	26	27	28	29	30
31						

AUGUST

MONDAY

25

Lefty birthday: Musician Elvis Costello

TUESDAY

26

Lefty birthday: Mother Teresa

WEDNESDAY

27

Lefty birthday: Formula One racer Gerhard Berger

THURSDAY

28

Lefty birthday: Author Johann Wolfgang von Goethe

FRIDAY

29

Lefty birthday: Former senator John McCain

SATURDAY

30

Lefty birthday: Cartoonist Robert Crumb

SUNDAY

31

☽ First Quarter
Lefty birthday: Olympic swimmer Ian Crocker

NAME THE LEFTY

Q: In what has become a classic cameo appearance, in the movie *Annie Hall,* a pompous academic is arguing with Woody Allen's character in a movie theater line. As fellow lefty Diane Keaton looks on, they are silenced by the sudden appearance of this intellectual southpaw, who says, "You know nothing of my work."
Can you name him?

A: Marshall McLuhan

September 2025

S	M	T	W	T	F	S
	1	2	3	4	5	6
7	8	9	10	11	12	13
14	15	16	17	18	19	20
21	22	23	24	25	26	27
28	29	30				

SEPTEMBER

MONDAY

1

Labor Day
Lefty birthday: Musician Sir Barry Gibb

TUESDAY

2

Lefty birthday: Tennis player Jimmy Connors

WEDNESDAY

3

Lefty birthday: Basketball coach Dick Motta

THURSDAY

4

Lefty birthday: Auto manufacturer Henry Ford II

FRIDAY

5

Lefty birthday: Cartoonist Cathy Guisewite

SATURDAY

6

Lefty birthday: Cricket player Saeed Anwar

SUNDAY

7

○ Full Moon
Lefty birthday: Figure skater Rudy Galindo

INSPIRATION FROM LEFTIES

I begin with an idea and then it becomes something else.

—Pablo Picasso

September 2025

S	M	T	W	T	F	S
	1	2	3	4	5	6
7	8	9	10	11	12	13
14	15	16	17	18	19	20
21	22	23	24	25	26	27
28	29	30				

SEPTEMBER

MONDAY

8

Lefty birthday: Comedian Sid Caesar

TUESDAY

9

Lefty birthday: Actor Henry Thomas

WEDNESDAY

10

Lefty birthday: Musician Joe Perry

THURSDAY

11

Lefty birthday: Actress Kristy McNichol

FRIDAY

12

Lefty birthday: Scientist Irène Joliot-Curie

SATURDAY

13

Lefty birthday: Singer Niall Horan

SUNDAY

14

◐ Last Quarter
Lefty birthday: Actor Walter Koenig

LEFTIES PLAYING LEFTIES

In the *Dick Van Dyke Show* episode "The Impractical Joke," Rob Petrie, played by left-handed actor Dick Van Dyke, mentions that he is left-handed.

September 2025

S	M	T	W	T	F	S
	1	2	3	4	5	6
7	8	9	10	11	12	13
14	15	16	17	18	19	20
21	22	23	24	25	26	27
28	29	30				

SEPTEMBER

MONDAY

15

Lefty birthday: Baseball player Nick Altrock

TUESDAY

16

Lefty birthday: Musician B. B. King

WEDNESDAY

17

Lefty birthday: Singer Hank Williams

THURSDAY

18

Lefty birthday: Actor Jason Sudeikis

FRIDAY

19

Lefty birthday: Songwriter Sylvia Tyson

SATURDAY

20

Lefty birthday: Comedienne Anne Meara

SUNDAY

21

● New Moon
Lefty birthday: Author H. G. Wells

Thirty-first president of the United States Herbert Hoover was born in Iowa, the first president to be born west of the Mississippi River. Orphaned at age nine, Hoover lived with a grandmother in Iowa and later with an uncle in Oregon. This lefty graduated with a degree in geology and became a professional mining engineer, a businessman, a worldwide humanitarian, director of the U.S. Food Administration, and secretary of commerce before winning the presidency. After leaving office, Hoover wrote articles and books and later served on government commissions under Presidents Harry S. Truman, a fellow lefty, and Dwight D. Eisenhower.

September 2025

S	M	T	W	T	F	S
	1	2	3	4	5	6
7	8	9	10	11	12	13
14	15	16	17	18	19	20
21	22	23	24	25	26	27
28	29	30				

SEPTEMBER

MONDAY

22

Autumnal Equinox
Rosh Hashanah begins at sundown
Lefty birthday: Musician Joan Jett

TUESDAY

23

Lefty birthday: Actor Jason Alexander

WEDNESDAY

24

Rosh Hashanah ends at sundown
Lefty birthday: Puppeteer Jim Henson

THURSDAY

25

Lefty birthday: Pianist Glenn Gould

FRIDAY

26

Lefty birthday: Actress Melissa Sue Anderson

SATURDAY

27

SUNDAY

28

Lefty birthday: Hockey player Grant Fuhr

Did you know that pets can be left-handed too? A 2019 study of paw preference in cats and dogs showed that 36 percent to 46 percent of cats were left pawed and that 31 percent to 53 percent of dogs were lefties.

September 2025

S	M	T	W	T	F	S
	1	2	3	4	5	6
7	8	9	10	11	12	13
14	15	16	17	18	19	20
21	22	23	24	25	26	27
28	29	30				

October 2025

S	M	T	W	T	F	S
			1	2	3	4
5	6	7	8	9	10	11
12	13	14	15	16	17	18
19	20	21	22	23	24	25
26	27	28	29	30	31	

SEP-OCT

MONDAY
29
◐ First Quarter
Lefty birthday: Sir Horatio Lord Nelson

TUESDAY
30
National Day for Truth and Reconciliation (Canada)
Lefty birthday: Actress Fran Drescher

WEDNESDAY
1
Yom Kippur begins at sundown
Lefty birthday: Baseball player Rod Carew

THURSDAY
2
Lefty birthday: Pacifist and nonviolence leader Mahatma Gandh

FRIDAY
3
Lefty birthday: Actress Rebecca Humphries

SATURDAY
4
Lefty birthday: Baseball player Charlie Leibrandt

SUNDAY
5
Lefty birthday: Musician and political activist Bob Geldof

INSPIRATION FROM LEFTIES

If it's worth using once, it's worth using twice.

—Tom Stoppard

October 2025

S	M	T	W	T	F	S
			1	2	3	4
5	6	7	8	9	10	11
12	13	14	15	16	17	18
19	20	21	22	23	24	25
26	27	28	29	30	31	

OCTOBER

MONDAY

6

Sukkot begins at sundown
Lefty birthday: Comedian Fred Travalena

TUESDAY

7

○ Full Moon
Lefty birthday: Bishop Desmond Tutu

WEDNESDAY

8

Lefty birthday: Author Walter Lord

THURSDAY

9

FRIDAY

10

Lefty birthday: Actress Sarah Lancashire

SATURDAY

11

Lefty birthday: Golfer Greg Chalmers

SUNDAY

12

Lefty birthday: Actor Hugh Jackman

Austin Krajicek was born in Florida and started playing tennis at age five. He won the U.S. national junior championships at eighteen and lettered at Texas A&M. Turning professional in 2015, this hard-hitting lefty won eleven career doubles titles on the Association of Tennis Professionals (ATP) Tour. Since partnering with Ivan Dodig in 2021, Krajicek has won one ATP Masters 1000 title at the 2023 Monte-Carlo Masters and his maiden Grand Slam title at the 2023 French Open, a victory that crowned him the ATP world No. 1 in June 2023.

October 2025

S	M	T	W	T	F	S
			1	2	3	4
5	6	7	8	9	10	11
12	13	14	15	16	17	18
19	20	21	22	23	24	25
26	27	28	29	30	31	

OCTOBER

MONDAY

13

◐ Last Quarter
Columbus Day
Indigenous Peoples' Day
Sukkot ends at sundown
Thanksgiving (Canada)
Lefty birthday: Comedian Lenny Bruce

TUESDAY

14

Lefty birthday: Pianist Gary Graffman

WEDNESDAY

15

Lefty birthday: Philosopher Friedrich Nietzsche

THURSDAY

16

Lefty birthday: Baseball player Bryce Harper

FRIDAY

17

Lefty birthday: Rapper Eminem

SATURDAY

18

Lefty birthday: Tennis player Martina Navratilova

SUNDAY

19

Lefty birthday: Actor and performer Divine

THE QUOTABLE LEFTY

I was a left-handed first baseman. I hit the ball pretty well. Then, I got into music, and I became a professional musician for a couple of years. . . . Clarinet, saxophone, flute, bass clarinet.

—Alan Greenspan, economist and former chairman of the Federal Reserve

October 2025

S	M	T	W	T	F	S
			1	2	3	4
5	6	7	8	9	10	11
12	13	14	15	16	17	18
19	20	21	22	23	24	25
26	27	28	29	30	31	

OCTOBER

MONDAY
20
Diwali
Lefty birthday: Actor Eric Scott

TUESDAY
21
● New Moon
Lefty birthday: Baseball player Edward "Whitey" Ford

WEDNESDAY
22
Lefty birthday: Musician Zac Hanson

THURSDAY
23
Lefty birthday: Soccer player Pelé

FRIDAY
24
Lefty birthday: Designer Zac Posen

SATURDAY
25
Lefty birthday: Artist Pablo Picasso

SUNDAY
26
Lefty birthday: Doctor and humanitarian Paul Farmer

FICTIONAL LEFTY

In the song "Ziggy Stardust," from the album *The Rise and Fall of Ziggy Stardust and the Spiders from Mars,* lyrics written by left-handed musician David Bowie state that "Ziggy Stardust played guitar . . . he played it left hand . . ."

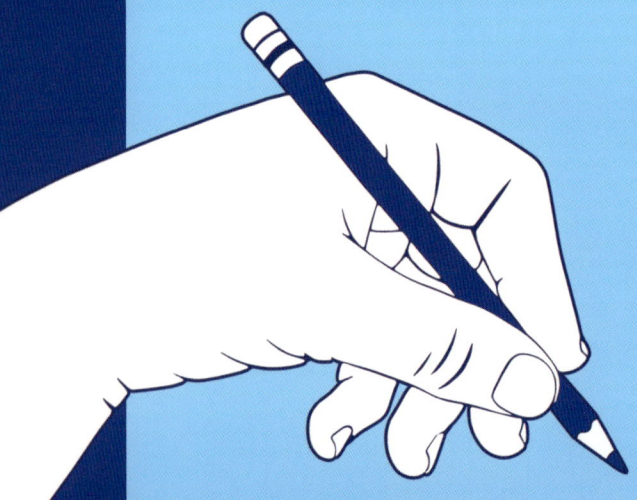

October 2025

S	M	T	W	T	F	S
			1	2	3	4
5	6	7	8	9	10	11
12	13	14	15	16	17	18
19	20	21	22	23	24	25
26	27	28	29	30	31	

November 2025

S	M	T	W	T	F	S
						1
2	3	4	5	6	7	8
9	10	11	12	13	14	15
16	17	18	19	20	21	22
23	24	25	26	27	28	29
30						

OCT-NOV

MONDAY
27

Lefty birthday: Journalist Terry Anderson

TUESDAY
28

Lefty birthday: Microsoft cofounder Bill Gates

WEDNESDAY
29

◐ First Quarter
Lefty birthday: Cartoonist Bill Mauldin

THURSDAY
30

Lefty birthday: Actor Leon Rippy

FRIDAY
31

Halloween
Lefty birthday: Golfer Russ Cochran

SATURDAY
1

Lefty birthday: Baseball player Fernando Valenzuela

SUNDAY
2

Daylight Saving Time ends
Lefty birthday: Drummer Carter Beauford

Riz Ahmed is a British Pakistani actor, rapper, musician, and activist. After graduating from Christ Church, Oxford University, with a degree in philosophy, politics, and economics, he studied acting at the Royal Central School of Speech and Drama. Among his film and television credits are *The Road to Guantanamo, Four Lions, The Reluctant Fundamentalist, Nightcrawler, The Night Of, Jason Bourne, Girls,* and *Sound of Metal,* for which he earned Golden Globe and Academy Award nominations. His Outstanding Lead Actor Emmy win for *The Night Of* made this lefty the first Asian male and the first Muslim to win a lead acting Emmy. In 2020, he produced, cowrote, and starred in *Mogul Mowgli,* which earned a nomination for the BAFTA Award for Outstanding British Film. As an activist, he is known for his political rap music that helps raise awareness and funds for refugee children.

November 2025

S	M	T	W	T	F	S
						1
2	3	4	5	6	7	8
9	10	11	12	13	14	15
16	17	18	19	20	21	22
23	24	25	26	27	28	29
30						

NOVEMBER

MONDAY

3

Lefty birthday: Actor Jeremy Brett

TUESDAY

4

Election Day
Lefty birthday: Chef Curtis Stone

WEDNESDAY

5

○ Full Moon
Lefty birthday: Basketball player Bill Walton

THURSDAY

6

Lefty birthday: Musician Glenn Frey

FRIDAY

7

Lefty birthday: Evangelist Billy Graham

SATURDAY

8

Lefty birthday: Chef Gordon Ramsay

SUNDAY

9

Lefty birthday: Soccer player Andreas Brehme

INSPIRATION FROM LEFTIES

Every one of us gets through the tough times because somebody is there, standing in the gap to close it for us.

—Oprah Winfrey

November 2025

S	M	T	W	T	F	S
						1
2	3	4	5	6	7	8
9	10	11	12	13	14	15
16	17	18	19	20	21	22
23	24	25	26	27	28	29
30						

NOVEMBER

MONDAY

10

Lefty birthday: King George II of England

TUESDAY

11

Veterans Day
Remembrance Day (Canada)

WEDNESDAY

12

◐ Last Quarter
Lefty birthday: Basketball player Russell Westbrook

THURSDAY

13

Lefty birthday: Comedienne and actress Whoopi Goldberg

FRIDAY

14

Lefty birthday: King Charles III of England

SATURDAY

15

Lefty birthday: Handball player Katarina Bulatović

SUNDAY

16

Lefty birthday: Emperor Tiberius

WHAT WERE THEIR NAMES BEFORE?

George Burns (Nathan Birnbaum)

Whoopi Goldberg (Caryn Johnson)

Demi Moore (Demi Guynes)

Jon Stewart (Jonathan Stuart Leibowitz)

November 2025						
S	M	T	W	T	F	S
						1
2	3	4	5	6	7	8
9	10	11	12	13	14	15
16	17	18	19	20	21	22
23	24	25	26	27	28	29
30						

NOVEMBER

MONDAY
17
Lefty birthday: Actor Rock Hudson

TUESDAY
18
Lefty birthday: Actor Owen Wilson

WEDNESDAY
19
Lefty birthday: Former president James Garfield

THURSDAY
20
● New Moon
Lefty birthday: Comedian Dick Smothers

FRIDAY
21
Lefty birthday: Baseball player Stan Musial

SATURDAY
22
Lefty birthday: Actress Scarlett Johansson

SUNDAY
23
Lefty birthday: Comedian Harpo Marx

THE LEFT STUFF

A lot of lefties find that using a can opener is annoying. Now you can have one made just for you! The Nogent Mini-Kim Can Opener has no moving parts, is made in France, and is guaranteed for life. Westmark Monopol Left-Handed Safety Can Opener and the Left-Handed Can Opener by Lefty's The Left Hand Store are both designed to be held by your right hand while your stronger left hand rotates counterclockwise.

November 2025

S	M	T	W	T	F	S
						1
2	3	4	5	6	7	8
9	10	11	12	13	14	15
16	17	18	19	20	21	22
23	24	25	26	27	28	29
30						

NOVEMBER

MONDAY
24

TUESDAY
25
Lefty birthday: Lawyer and publisher John F. Kennedy Jr.

WEDNESDAY
26
Lefty birthday: Baseball player Vernon "Lefty" Gomez

THURSDAY
27
Thanksgiving
Lefty birthday: Musician Jimi Hendrix

FRIDAY
28
◐ First Quarter
Lefty birthday: Actress Hope Lange

SATURDAY
29
Lefty birthday: Writer and director Joel Coen

SUNDAY
30
Lefty birthday: Former prime minister Sir Winston Churchill

Born and raised in South Bend, Indiana, Pete Buttigieg went on to become mayor of South Bend in 2012 and a 2020 presidential candidate. This lefty politician was valedictorian of his high school, graduated from Harvard University magna cum laude, was awarded a Rhodes Scholarship, and graduated with first-class honors from Pembroke College, Oxford. Buttigieg also became an ensign in the Navy Reserves and served as a counterintelligence officer in Afghanistan for seven months in 2014. On February 3, 2021, he became the youngest person ever to serve as U.S. secretary of transportation.

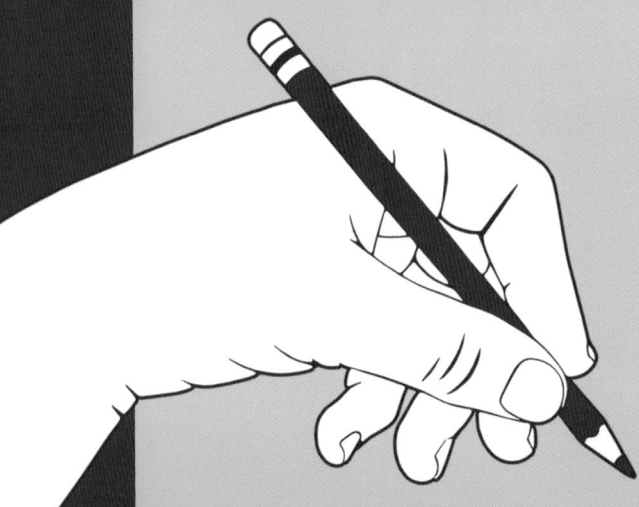

December 2025

S	M	T	W	T	F	S
	1	2	3	4	5	6
7	8	9	10	11	12	13
14	15	16	17	18	19	20
21	22	23	24	25	26	27
28	29	30	31			

DECEMBER

MONDAY

1

Lefty birthday: Singer Lou Rawls

TUESDAY

2

Lefty birthday: Tennis player Monica Seles

WEDNESDAY

3

Lefty birthday: Actress Julianne Moore

THURSDAY

4

○ Full Moon
Lefty birthday: Author Thomas Carlyle

FRIDAY

5

SATURDAY

6

SUNDAY

7

Lefty birthday: Basketball player Larry Bird

LEFTY OR NOT?

Former president Gerald Ford reportedly wrote left-handed when sitting down and right-handed when standing up!

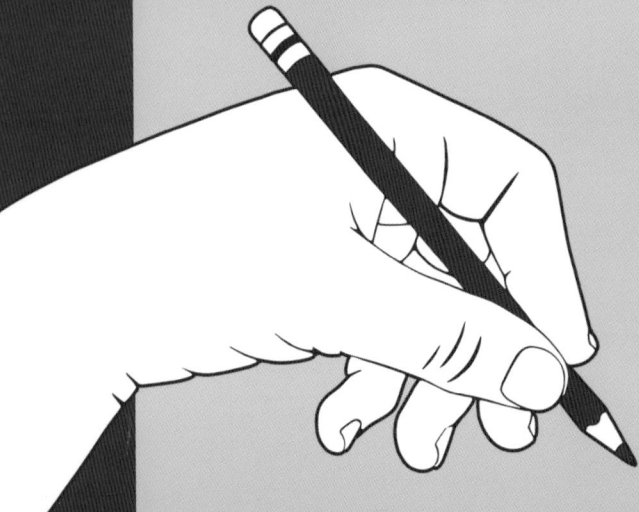

December 2025

S	M	T	W	T	F	S
	1	2	3	4	5	6
7	8	9	10	11	12	13
14	15	16	17	18	19	20
21	22	23	24	25	26	27
28	29	30	31			

DECEMBER

MONDAY

8

Lefty birthday: Actress Kim Basinger

TUESDAY

9

Lefty birthday: Football player David Akers

WEDNESDAY

10

Lefty birthday: Baseball player Paul Assenmacher

THURSDAY

11

◑ Last Quarter
Lefty birthday: Activist and politician Tom Hayden

FRIDAY

12

Lefty birthday: Painter Edvard Munch

SATURDAY

13

Lefty birthday: Actor Dick Van Dyke

SUNDAY

14

Hanukkah begins at sundown
Lefty birthday: King George VI of England

INSPIRATION FROM LEFTIES

Life belongs to the living, and he who lives must be prepared for change.

—Johann Wolfgang von Goethe

December 2025						
S	M	T	W	T	F	S
	1	2	3	4	5	6
7	8	9	10	11	12	13
14	15	16	17	18	19	20
21	22	23	24	25	26	27
28	29	30	31			

DECEMBER

MONDAY
15
Lefty birthday: Baseball player Mo Vaughn

TUESDAY
16
Lefty birthday: Baseball player Mike Flanagan

WEDNESDAY
17
Lefty birthday: Actress Milla Jovovich

THURSDAY
18
Lefty birthday: Painter Paul Klee

FRIDAY
19
Lefty birthday: Drummer Lenny White

SATURDAY
20
● New Moon
Lefty birthday: Infanta Elena, Duchess of Lugo

SUNDAY
21
Winter Solstice
Lefty birthday: Baseball player Dorothy Kamenshek

CHARITABLE LEFTY

Basketball star LeBron James supports the Boys & Girls Clubs of America as well as several other charities focused on helping underprivileged children. This southpaw established the LeBron James Family Foundation, which raises and donates money to a variety of charities to help at-risk kids in the area of Akron, Ohio, James's hometown, with after-school programs, mentoring, education, and scholarships to the University of Akron when kids are college age. In 2018, he funded the building of the I Promise School in Akron for at-risk kids.

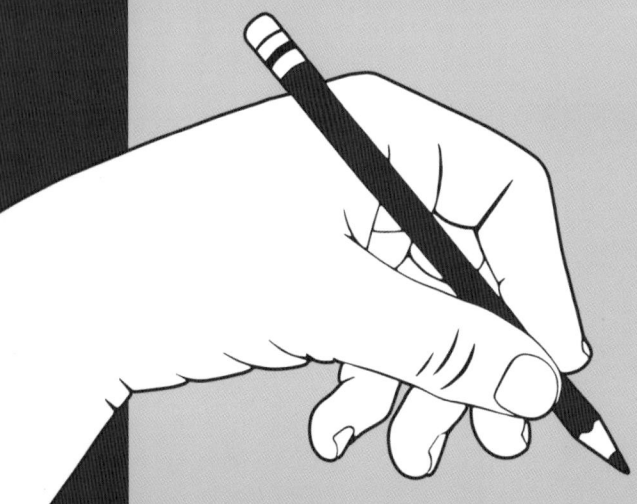

December 2025

S	M	T	W	T	F	S
	1	2	3	4	5	6
7	8	9	10	11	12	13
14	15	16	17	18	19	20
21	22	23	24	25	26	27
28	29	30	31			

DECEMBER

MONDAY
22
Hanukkah ends at sundown
Lefty birthday: Baseball player Steve Carlton

TUESDAY
23

WEDNESDAY
24
Lefty birthday: Singer Ricky Martin

THURSDAY
25
Christmas
Lefty birthday: Singer Annie Lennox

FRIDAY
26
Kwanzaa begins
Boxing Day (Canada)
Lefty birthday: Tennis player Marcelo Ríos

SATURDAY
27
☽ First Quarter
Lefty birthday: Television host Savannah Guthrie

SUNDAY
28
Lefty birthday: Comic book writer and producer Stan Lee

YOU'VE COME A LONG WAY, LEFTY

- Today, if you choose to write with your left hand, in most schools you'll be encouraged, not switched.

- Once scarce, left-handed scissors are now common in kindergarten.

- No one raises an eyebrow when you request the outside left-handed place setting in a restaurant or at a dinner party.

December 2025						
S	M	T	W	T	F	S
	1	2	3	4	5	6
7	8	9	10	11	12	13
14	15	16	17	18	19	20
21	22	23	24	25	26	27
28	29	30	31			

January 2026						
S	M	T	W	T	F	S
				1	2	3
4	5	6	7	8	9	10
11	12	13	14	15	16	17
18	19	20	21	22	23	24
25	26	27	28	29	30	31

DEC '25–JAN '26

MONDAY
29
Lefty birthday: Cellist Pablo Casals

TUESDAY
30
Lefty birthday: Basketball player LeBron James

WEDNESDAY
31
Lefty birthday: Actor Val Kilmer

THURSDAY
1
New Year's Day
Kwanzaa ends
Lefty birthday: Actor Frank Langella

FRIDAY
2
Lefty birthday: Actress Renée Elise Goldsberry

SATURDAY
3
○ Full Moon
Lefty birthday: Hockey player Bobby Hull

SUNDAY
4
Lefty birthday: Physicist Sir Isaac Newton

JULY

AUGUST

SEPTEMBER

OCTOBER

NOVEMBER

DECEMBER

2026

JANUARY

FEBRUARY

MARCH

APRIL

MAY

JUNE

2024

January
S	M	T	W	T	F	S
	1	2	3	4	5	6
7	8	9	10	11	12	13
14	15	16	17	18	19	20
21	22	23	24	25	26	27
28	29	30	31			

February
S	M	T	W	T	F	S
				1	2	3
4	5	6	7	8	9	10
11	12	13	14	15	16	17
18	19	20	21	22	23	24
25	26	27	28	29		

March
S	M	T	W	T	F	S
					1	2
3	4	5	6	7	8	9
10	11	12	13	14	15	16
17	18	19	20	21	22	23
24	25	26	27	28	29	30
31						

April
S	M	T	W	T	F	S
	1	2	3	4	5	6
7	8	9	10	11	12	13
14	15	16	17	18	19	20
21	22	23	24	25	26	27
28	29	30				

May
S	M	T	W	T	F	S
			1	2	3	4
5	6	7	8	9	10	11
12	13	14	15	16	17	18
19	20	21	22	23	24	25
26	27	28	29	30	31	

June
S	M	T	W	T	F	S
						1
2	3	4	5	6	7	8
9	10	11	12	13	14	15
16	17	18	19	20	21	22
23	24	25	26	27	28	29
30						

July
S	M	T	W	T	F	S
	1	2	3	4	5	6
7	8	9	10	11	12	13
14	15	16	17	18	19	20
21	22	23	24	25	26	27
28	29	30	31			

August
S	M	T	W	T	F	S
				1	2	3
4	5	6	7	8	9	10
11	12	13	14	15	16	17
18	19	20	21	22	23	24
25	26	27	28	29	30	31

September
S	M	T	W	T	F	S
1	2	3	4	5	6	7
8	9	10	11	12	13	14
15	16	17	18	19	20	21
22	23	24	25	26	27	28
29	30					

October
S	M	T	W	T	F	S
		1	2	3	4	5
6	7	8	9	10	11	12
13	14	15	16	17	18	19
20	21	22	23	24	25	26
27	28	29	30	31		

November
S	M	T	W	T	F	S
					1	2
3	4	5	6	7	8	9
10	11	12	13	14	15	16
17	18	19	20	21	22	23
24	25	26	27	28	29	30

December
S	M	T	W	T	F	S
1	2	3	4	5	6	7
8	9	10	11	12	13	14
15	16	17	18	19	20	21
22	23	24	25	26	27	28
29	30	31				

2026

January
S	M	T	W	T	F	S
				1	2	3
4	5	6	7	8	9	10
11	12	13	14	15	16	17
18	19	20	21	22	23	24
25	26	27	28	29	30	31

February
S	M	T	W	T	F	S
1	2	3	4	5	6	7
8	9	10	11	12	13	14
15	16	17	18	19	20	21
22	23	24	25	26	27	28

March
S	M	T	W	T	F	S
1	2	3	4	5	6	7
8	9	10	11	12	13	14
15	16	17	18	19	20	21
22	23	24	25	26	27	28
29	30	31				

April
S	M	T	W	T	F	S
			1	2	3	4
5	6	7	8	9	10	11
12	13	14	15	16	17	18
19	20	21	22	23	24	25
26	27	28	29	30		

May
S	M	T	W	T	F	S
					1	2
3	4	5	6	7	8	9
10	11	12	13	14	15	16
17	18	19	20	21	22	23
24	25	26	27	28	29	30
31						

June
S	M	T	W	T	F	S
	1	2	3	4	5	6
7	8	9	10	11	12	13
14	15	16	17	18	19	20
21	22	23	24	25	26	27
28	29	30				

July
S	M	T	W	T	F	S
			1	2	3	4
5	6	7	8	9	10	11
12	13	14	15	16	17	18
19	20	21	22	23	24	25
26	27	28	29	30	31	

August
S	M	T	W	T	F	S
						1
2	3	4	5	6	7	8
9	10	11	12	13	14	15
16	17	18	19	20	21	22
23	24	25	26	27	28	29
30	31					

September
S	M	T	W	T	F	S
		1	2	3	4	5
6	7	8	9	10	11	12
13	14	15	16	17	18	19
20	21	22	23	24	25	26
27	28	29	30			

October
S	M	T	W	T	F	S
				1	2	3
4	5	6	7	8	9	10
11	12	13	14	15	16	17
18	19	20	21	22	23	24
25	26	27	28	29	30	31

November
S	M	T	W	T	F	S
1	2	3	4	5	6	7
8	9	10	11	12	13	14
15	16	17	18	19	20	21
22	23	24	25	26	27	28
29	30					

December
S	M	T	W	T	F	S
		1	2	3	4	5
6	7	8	9	10	11	12
13	14	15	16	17	18	19
20	21	22	23	24	25	26
27	28	29	30	31		